The Comprehensive Collection of Things That Jon Snow Knows

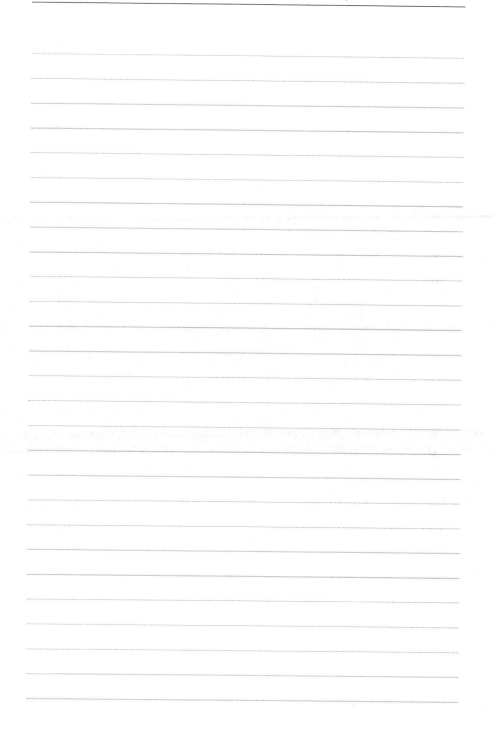

55081622R00091

Made in the USA
Lexington, KY
09 September 2016

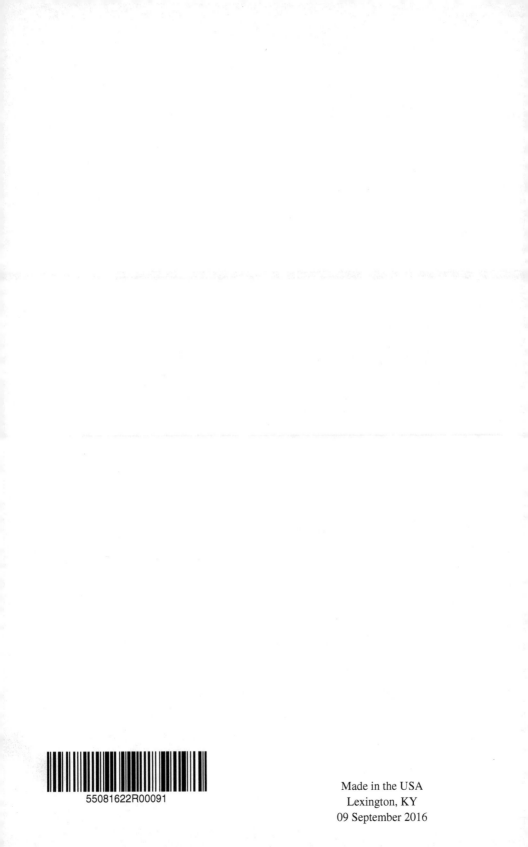